It's J!

Mary Elizabeth Salzmann

Consulting Editor, Diane Craig, M.A./Reading Specialist

Published by ABDO Publishing Company, 8000 West 78th Street, Edina, Minnesota 55439. Copyright © 2010 by Abdo Consulting Group, Inc. International copyrights reserved in all countries. No part of this book may be reproduced in any form without written permission from the publisher. Super SandCastle™ is a trademark and logo of ABDO Publishing Company.

Printed in the United States.

♻ PRINTED ON RECYCLED PAPER

Editor: Pam Price
Content Developer: Nancy Tuminelly
Cover and Interior Design and Production: Kelly Doudna, Mighty Media
Photo Credits: Brand X Pictures, iStockphoto (Monika Adamczyk, Jani Bryson, Peggy De Meue), Photodisc, Shutterstock

Library of Congress Cataloging-in-Publication Data
Salzmann, Mary Elizabeth, 1968-
  It's J! / Mary Elizabeth Salzmann.
     p. cm. -- (It's the alphabet!)
  ISBN 978-1-60453-597-6
  1. English language--Alphabet--Juvenile literature. 2. Alphabet books--Juvenile literature. I. Title.
  PE1155.S268 2010
  421'.1--dc22
  ⟨E⟩
                              2009020955

Super SandCastle™ books are created by a team of professional educators, reading specialists, and content developers around five essential components—phonemic awareness, phonics, vocabulary, text comprehension, and fluency—to assist young readers as they develop reading skills and strategies and increase their general knowledge. All books are written, reviewed, and leveled for guided reading, early reading intervention, and Accelerated Reader® programs for use in shared, guided, and independent reading and writing activities to support a balanced approach to literacy instruction.

About SUPER SANDCASTLE™

**Bigger Books for Emerging Readers
Grades K–4**

Created for library, classroom, and at-home use, Super SandCastle™ books support and engage young readers as they develop and build literacy skills and will increase their general knowledge about the world around them. Super SandCastle™ books are an extension of SandCastle™, the leading preK–3 imprint for emerging and beginning readers. Super SandCastle™ features a larger trim size for more reading fun.

Let Us Know
Super SandCastle™ would like to hear your stories about reading this book. What was your favorite page? Was there something hard that you needed help with? Share the ups and downs of learning to read. We want to hear from you! Send us an e-mail.

sandcastle@abdopublishing.com

Contact us for a complete list of SandCastle™, Super SandCastle™, and other nonfiction and fiction titles from ABDO Publishing Company.

www.abdopublishing.com • 8000 West 78th Street
Edina, MN 55439 • 800-800-1312 • 952-831-1632 fax

Aa Bb Cc Dd Ee
Ff Gg Hh Ii Jj Kk
Ll Mm Nn Oo Pp
Qq Rr Ss Tt Uu Vv
Ww Xx Yy Zz

The Letter

Jj

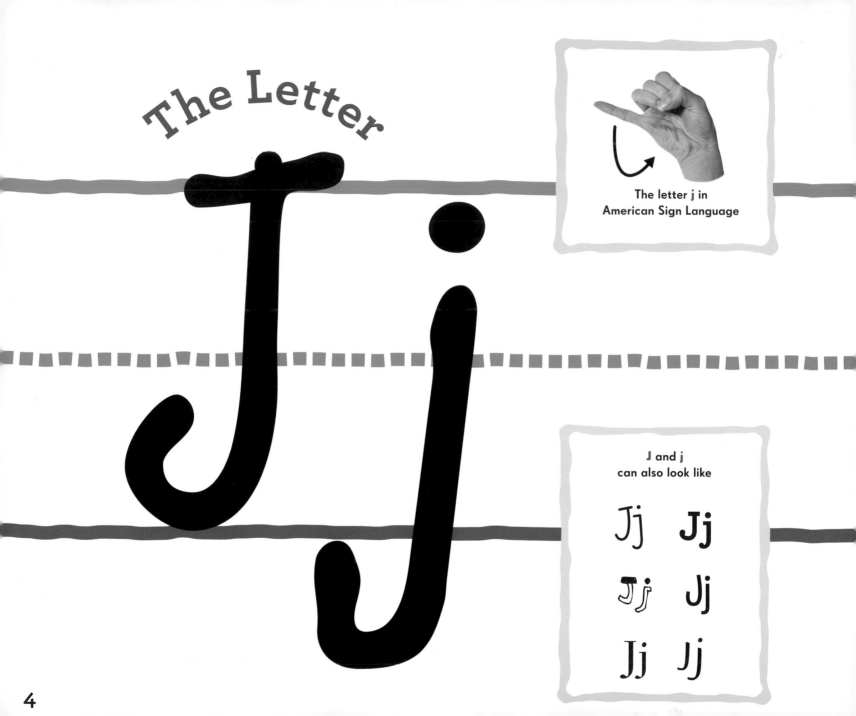

The letter j in
American Sign Language

J and j
can also look like

Jj **Jj**

𝕁𝕛 Jj

Jj Jj

The letter j is a consonant.

It is the 10th letter of the alphabet.

Some words start with **j**.

jeans

jacket

6

Julie

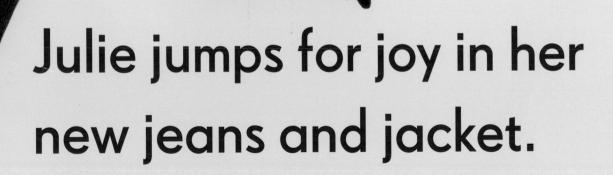

Julie jumps for joy in her new jeans and jacket.

jet

jar

jam

Jessica

Jessica juggles jars of jam on a jet.

☞ Some words have
j in the middle.

pajamas

banjo

Benjamin

Benjamin enjoys playing the banjo in his pajamas.

In Spanish words, the letter j sounds like an h.

fajita

jalapeño

San Jose

California

12

Juan

Juan eats fajitas with jalapeños in San Jose.

13

My friend Jen lives in San Jose.

She juggles jewels for hours each day.

When Jen juggles, she wears blue jeans.

Her favorite snack is jelly beans.

"I'm tired of juggling jewels," says Jen.

"I'll juggle something else now and then."

Jen juggles banjos and then jars of jam.

She even juggles jellyfish and a jumbo clam.

Jen jumps into her pajamas that night.

She thinks, "Some objects just don't juggle right."

Jelly beans!

T.J. gives Jen an idea the next day.

She could juggle jelly beans in San Jose!

San Jose

●San Jose

California

Which words have
the letter j?

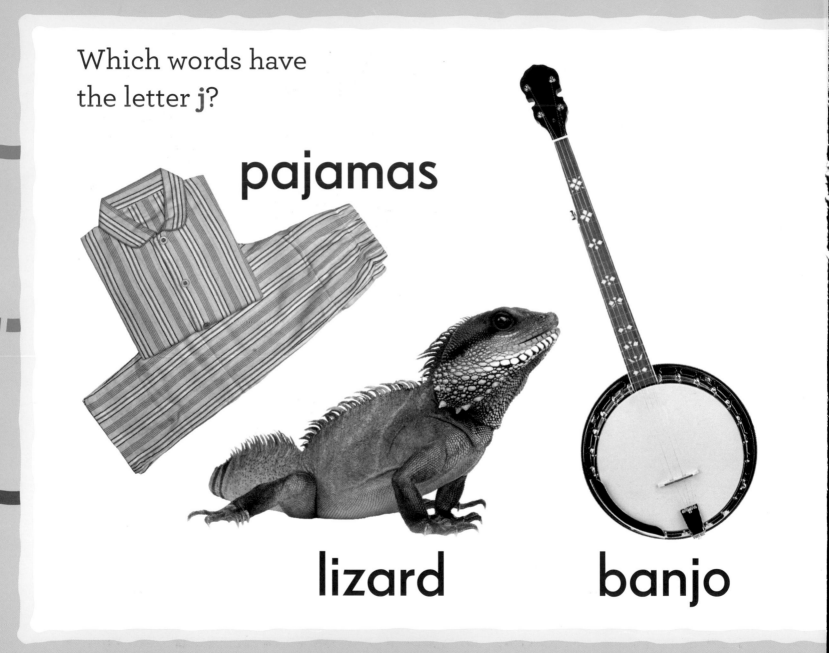

pajamas

lizard

banjo

comb

jacket

jeans

jam

dog

23

Glossary

banjo (pp. 10, 11, 18, 22) – a musical instrument with a round body, a long neck, and four or five strings.

fajita (pp. 12, 13) – a dish of grilled meat served in a tortilla with peppers and onions.

favorite (p. 16) – someone or something that you like best.

jalapeño (pp. 12, 13) – a kind of green chili pepper grown in Mexico and the southern United States.

jellyfish (p. 18) – a sea creature with a soft body and a lot of tentacles.

jewel (pp. 15, 17) – a precious stone such as an emerald or a diamond.

juggle (pp. 9, 15, 16, 17, 18, 19, 20) – to toss several objects from hand to hand so that they are always moving.

jumbo (p. 18) – larger than most things of the same kind.

To promote letter recognition, letters are highlighted instead of glossary words in this series. The page numbers above indicate where the glossary words can be found.

More Words with J

Find the **j** in the beginning or middle of each word.

adjective	Japan	join	jug	majesty
ajar	jeep	joke	juice	major
injure	jelly	jot	July	objective
jab	jingle	journal	June	project
jack	job	journey	junk	reject
January	jog	judge	Jupiter	subject